CONTENTS

WHAT WAS A HOPLITE?

A hoplite was a type of ancient Greek soldier. Hoplites fought on foot and were the most important men in Greek armies.

Military life

Soldiers, including hoplites, in ancient Greece did not usually belong to a full-time army. They had jobs when they were not at war.

> Most hoplites came from wealthy families who could afford to buy the weapons and armour they needed.

GREEK WARRIOR

Deborah Murrell

ISBN 978 1 84835 232 2

Author Deborah Murrell
Consultant Philip Steele
Project Editor Eve Marleau
Designer and Picture Researcher
  Andrew McGovern
Illustrator Peter Dennis

Publisher Steve Evans
Creative Director Zeta Davies
Managing Editor Amanda Askew

Printed and bound in China

Picture credits
Key: t=top, b=bottom, r=right, l=left, c=centre
Alamy 6–7 North Wind Picture Archives,
7b INTERFOTO/Personalities, 9t North Wind
Picture Archives, 10b North Wind Picture
Archives, 11r Maurice Crooks, 18b North
Wind Picture Archives, 19b Mary Evans
Picture Library
Bridgeman 4–5 Roger Payne, 5t Peter
Jackson, 6l Harry Green, 12c Italian School,
13c Andrew Howat, 13–14 Roger Payne,
20–21 James Edwin McConnell, 26l Peter
Jackson, 27t O'Shea Gallery, London,
27b Graham Coton
Corbis 16b Bettmann, 17c Bettmann,
23b Bettmann
Getty Images 28–29 Paul Avis
Johnny Shumate Illustration 5b, 14–15, 19,
21t, 22, 23t, 24–25
Photolibrary 13b The Print Collector
Topfoto 29c The Granger Collection

The words in **bold**
are explained in the
glossary on page 30.

SPARTANS

After 700 BC, the southern Greek city of Sparta began to take over the surrounding region called Lakonia. The Spartans made the people from the villages do their work, such as farming. The Spartans became full-time soldiers. Soon they were the most feared army in ancient Greece.

Poorer soldiers

Men from poorer families also fought in Greek armies. They could not afford the weapons and armour to become hoplites, and so they fought as **archers** or with **slings** and stones.

➢ *Poorer soldiers often fought with long-distance weapons, such as stones or bows and arrows.*

WHEN DID HOPLITES LIVE?

Ancient Greece was not a united country, as Greece is today, but made up of city-states. Armies often fought over territories. Hoplites were the main force in Greek armies between 600 and 300 BC.

Athens versus Sparta

Athens and Sparta were two of the strongest city-states in ancient Greece. Athens made a lot of money by trading, and it had a large navy to protect its sea routes. Sparta had a very strong land army, based around its hoplites.

⌃ *The Parthenon was the temple of Athene. This goddess was believed to protect the city of Athens.*

Greek armies

In ancient times, warriors with shields and spears often fought as a line formation to break through enemy front lines. The Greek city-states perfected this way of fighting, which they called a **phalanx**.

ILLYRIA

MACEDONIA

Athens and Sparta were two of the most powerful city-states.

Black Sea

THRACE

Byzantium •
Sea of Marmara

CHALCIDICE

THESSALY

EPIRUS

Corfu

PHRYGIA

MYSIA

Aegean Sea

AETOLIA

LOCRIS

PHOCIS **Delphi**

ANATOLIA

BOEOTIA

ATTICA

ACHAEA

LYDIA

Corinth   • **Athens**

Ionian Sea

Peloponnese

CARIA

Cyclades

IONIA

Dodecanese

LYCIA

LACONIA   • **Sparta**

Rhodes

Greek soldiers fought off Persian invaders at the Battle of Plataea in 479 BC.

AESCHYLUS
(c.525–456 BC)

Aeschylus was one of the greatest Greek writers. He fought in a famous battle at Marathon, near Athens. This is mentioned on his grave, but his plays are not!

TRAINING TO BE A HOPLITE

Hoplites throughout ancient Greece fought in much the same way, so they learned similar techniques. Hoplites were trained to work together as a team in a phalanx.

Boarding school

At about seven years old, Spartan boys were sent to boarding school to train to be hoplites. They learned many skills, including how to hunt and dance. They were not given much food, so they had to look after themselves. This often meant stealing from the other boys. The boys were not punished for stealing, but for being caught doing it.

▲ Spartan boys exercised to help them stay strong and fit.

Daily practice

Activities such as athletics contests helped hoplites gain the skills and strength they needed for battles. Spartan boys also had to learn poems by heart and read the work of great Greek philosophers, or thinkers.

◄ Spartan boys practised with wooden spears and shields, and were carefully watched over by their teachers.

WARRIOR WISDOM

At about 20 years old, Spartan men became members of a dining club. This was a special club where a small group of men would eat together. The club taught the men to rely on and trust each other. It was only after training and club membership that a man became a hoplite.

WEAPONS AND ARMOUR

Helmet

The most important part of a hoplite's armour was his shield. In the battle formation, or phalanx, the shield protected the hoplite holding it and the man to his left.

Chest armour

Shields

Hoplites carried large, round shields, made of wood or **bronze**. Shields were carried on the left arm so the right arm was free for fighting. The fighting arm was also protected by the shield of the man to the right in a phalanx.

➤The length of the hoplites' spears kept the enemy at a safe distance in the early stages of battle.

Greave

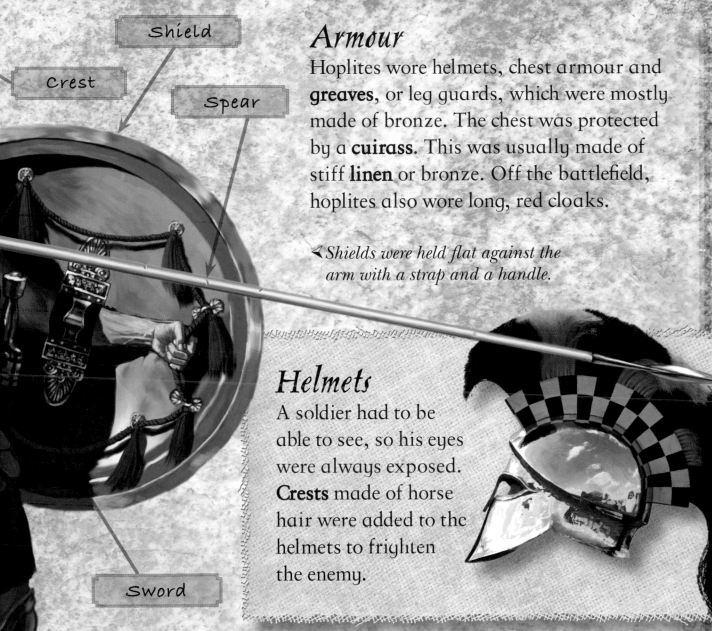

Shield

Crest

Spear

Armour

Hoplites wore helmets, chest armour and **greaves**, or leg guards, which were mostly made of bronze. The chest was protected by a **cuirass**. This was usually made of stiff **linen** or bronze. Off the battlefield, hoplites also wore long, red cloaks.

◄ *Shields were held flat against the arm with a strap and a handle.*

Helmets

A soldier had to be able to see, so his eyes were always exposed. **Crests** made of horse hair were added to the helmets to frighten the enemy.

Sword

Spears and swords

Spears were about 3 metres long and pointed at both ends. The bottom point of the spear could be stuck into the ground. The spear would then be held and pointed forwards during an attack. If the spear was broken or dropped, the hoplite fought with his sword.

◤ *Hoplites' helmets were often made of bronze.*

WAR MACHINES

For hoplites, the main tactic was to fight in a phalanx. Battles were often won by pushing the enemy off the battlefield. However, other kinds of tactics were also used.

➤ *Greek ships usually had both sails and oars. In battle, or if there was no wind, men used the oars to power the ship.*

⌃ *Battering rams were used to break down walls. Catapults threw torches into the city.*

Under siege

Sieges, or attacks on cities, were not very common in ancient Greece. When they did happen, various tactics were used. Hoplites sometimes used ladders, for example, to climb up enemy walls. However, the best weapons in a siege were large machines, such as **battering rams** and **catapults**.

All at sea

The most useful kind of warship in ancient Greece was called a **trireme**. Its name means 'three oars', as it had three banks of oars on each side. It also had a battering ram on the front. Triremes did not carry many soldiers – the ship itself was the main weapon.

SHIP SHAKER

Many Greek cities were on the coast. In 214 BC, after the time of hoplites, a scientist named Archimedes invented a useful machine. A large hook was lowered from a crane, and hooked under the enemy ship. Oxen pulled the ship out of the water. When the rope was released, the ship crashed into the water and sank.

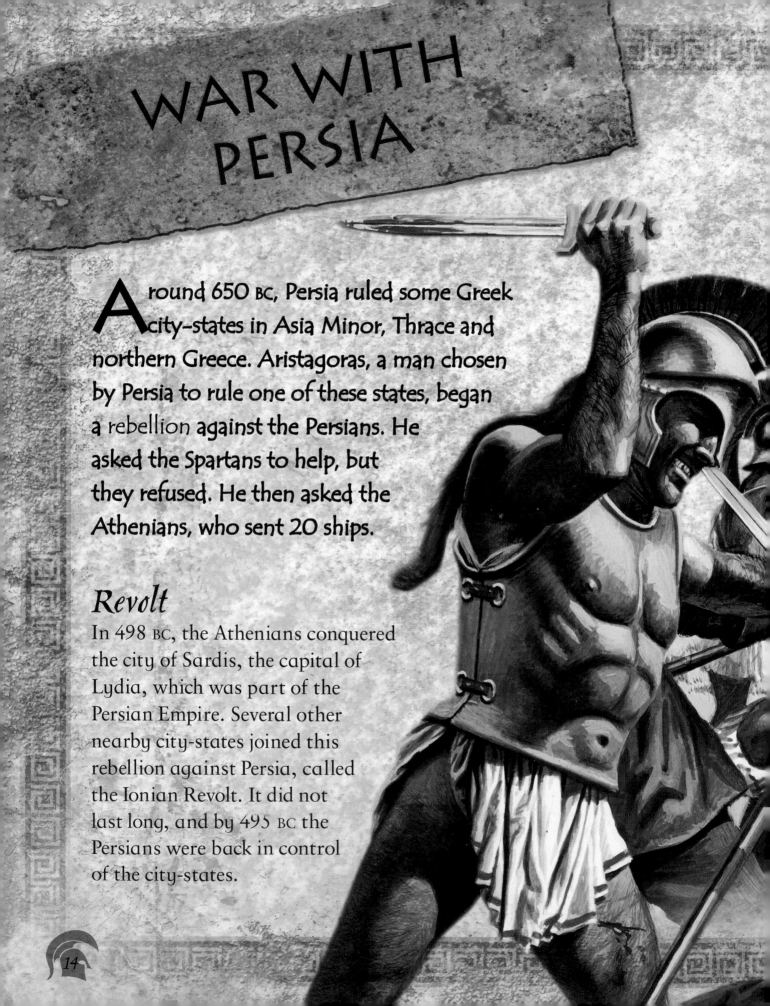

WAR WITH PERSIA

A round 650 BC, Persia ruled some Greek city-states in Asia Minor, Thrace and northern Greece. Aristagoras, a man chosen by Persia to rule one of these states, began a rebellion against the Persians. He asked the Spartans to help, but they refused. He then asked the Athenians, who sent 20 ships.

Revolt

In 498 BC, the Athenians conquered the city of Sardis, the capital of Lydia, which was part of the Persian Empire. Several other nearby city-states joined this rebellion against Persia, called the Ionian Revolt. It did not last long, and by 495 BC the Persians were back in control of the city-states.

The Battle of Marathon

The Persians did not forget the part Athens had played in the Ionian Revolt and, in 490 BC, they attacked Athens. The two armies met at Marathon, north of Athens. The Athenians were led by Miltiades, a soldier who had fought in the Persian army and knew how to beat them. He led the Athenians to victory.

▼ *Greeks and Persians fought a long and bloody battle at Marathon, near Athens.*

WARRIOR WISDOM

After the Battle of Marathon, a runner was sent to take the news of victory to Athens. He ran the 41 kilometres in armour. It is thought that he died just after passing on his message. Marathons are named after this event.

THE PERSIANS RETURN

In 481 BC, the Persians attacked again. Their king, Xerxes, wanted to conquer the whole of Greece. At the Battle of Thermopylae in 480 BC, a small army of hoplites led by the Spartans fought bravely against a much larger Persian army. The Spartans were defeated, but they held the Persians back for long enough to allow a much larger Greek army to prepare to fight them.

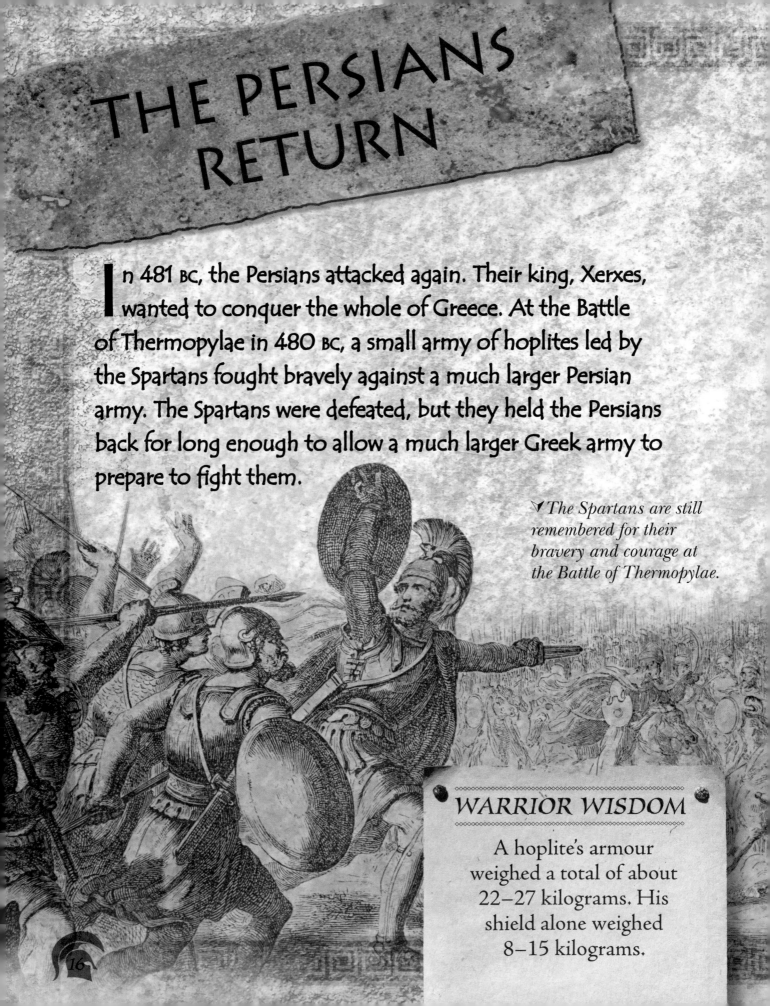

▾ *The Spartans are still remembered for their bravery and courage at the Battle of Thermopylae.*

WARRIOR WISDOM

A hoplite's armour weighed a total of about 22–27 kilograms. His shield alone weighed 8–15 kilograms.

The Battle of Salamis

When Xerxes and his army came to attack a month after Thermopylae, the Athenians had a fleet of ships, and were ready for them. In a battle off the island of Salamis, the Greeks beat the Persian fleet.

Peace at last

Although they had defeated the Persians, many Greeks feared they might return. The Athenians' victory meant many of the other city-states relied on Athens' ships to protect them. This made Athens very powerful. Sparta was also powerful, and the Spartans became jealous and suspicious of Athens.

➤ *The Battle of Salamis was the battle that won the Persian War for the Greeks.*

DEFEAT OF THE SPARTANS

After the Persian Wars, the city-states of ancient Greece continued to fight. Athens and Sparta led groups of city-states called leagues. Each league wanted to take control of more land. This fight for control was called the Peloponnesian War.

▼ *Sometimes both sails and oars were needed to control a ship.*

War between states

The Peloponnesian War began in 431 BC. At first, the Delian League, led by Athens' army, won many battles with their strong navy. Eventually, they surrendered to the Peloponnesian League, led by Sparta, in 404 BC.

Battle of Leuctra

Fighting between city-states did not stop. One of the most important battles took place at Leuctra in 371 BC between Sparta and Thebes. The Spartan hoplites were arranged in phalanxes of 8–12 lines, with the strongest fighters on the right. The Thebans attacked on the right with **cavalry** and 50 lines of hoplites. The Spartans, seeing their strongest men beaten, left the battlefield.

▽ *Before a battle, hoplites carried their spears pointing upwards.*

PHILIP II
(c.525–456 BC)

The Thebans did not have long to enjoy their victory. Greece was soon invaded by the army of Philip II of Macedonia, in the north of Greece.

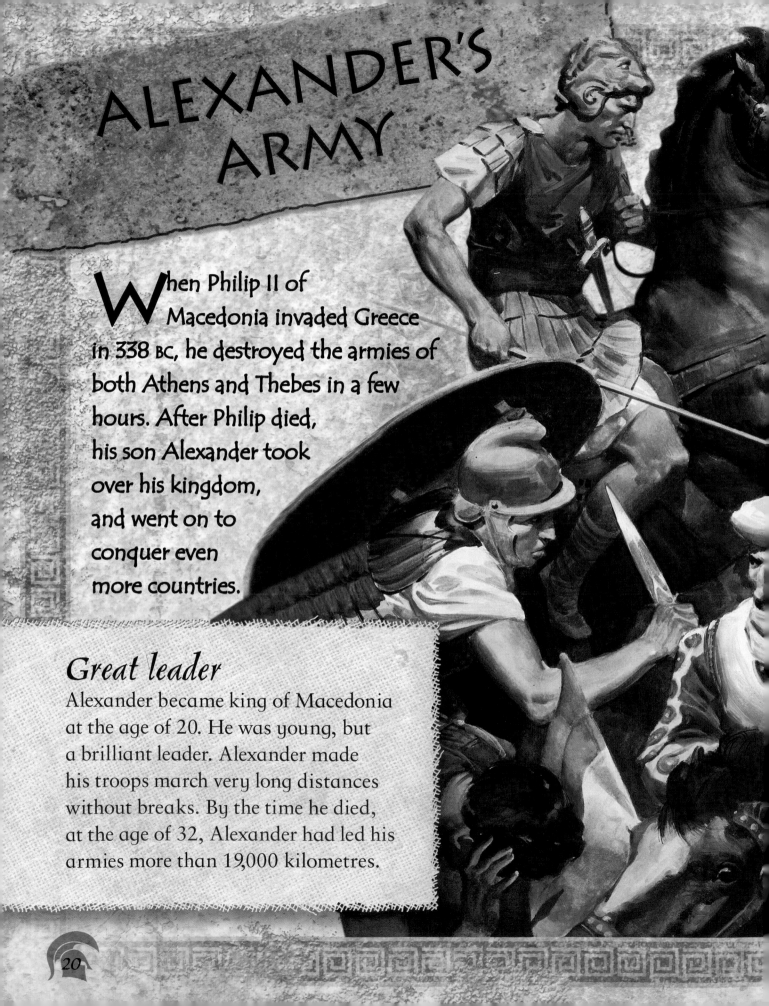

ALEXANDER'S ARMY

When Philip II of Macedonia invaded Greece in 338 BC, he destroyed the armies of both Athens and Thebes in a few hours. After Philip died, his son Alexander took over his kingdom, and went on to conquer even more countries.

Great leader

Alexander became king of Macedonia at the age of 20. He was young, but a brilliant leader. Alexander made his troops march very long distances without breaks. By the time he died, at the age of 32, Alexander had led his armies more than 19,000 kilometres.

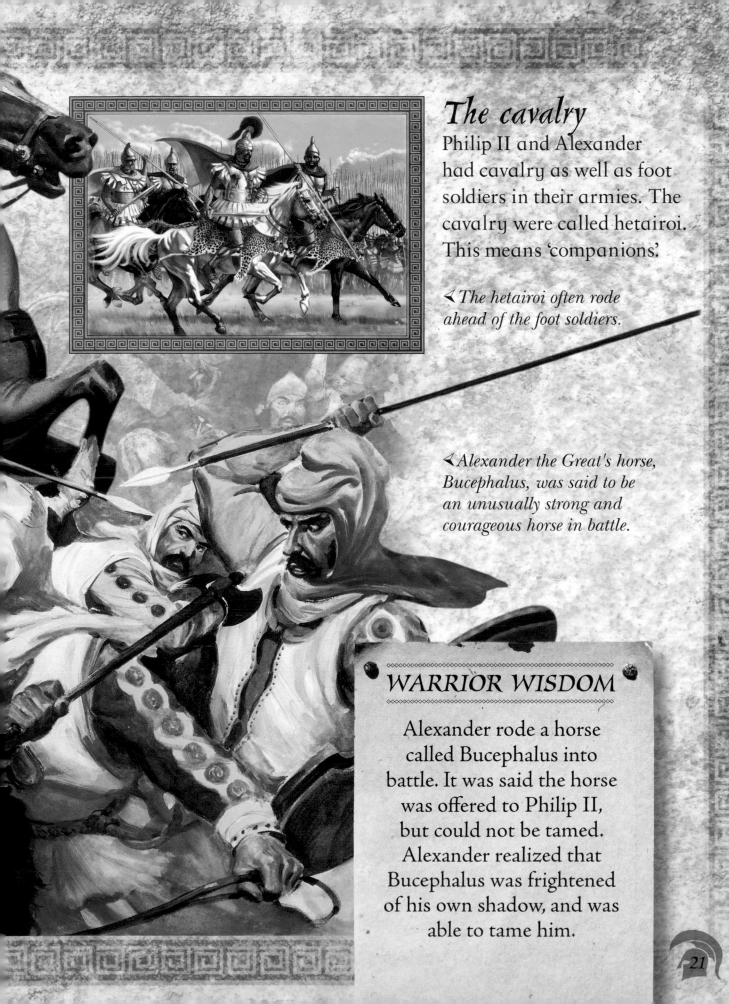

The cavalry

Philip II and Alexander had cavalry as well as foot soldiers in their armies. The cavalry were called hetairoi. This means 'companions'.

◄ *The hetairoi often rode ahead of the foot soldiers.*

◄ *Alexander the Great's horse, Bucephalus, was said to be an unusually strong and courageous horse in battle.*

WARRIOR WISDOM

Alexander rode a horse called Bucephalus into battle. It was said the horse was offered to Philip II, but could not be tamed. Alexander realized that Bucephalus was frightened of his own shadow, and was able to tame him.

MACEDONIAN WEAPONS AND ARMOUR

The army of ancient northern Greece, or Macedonia, was one of the greatest in the world. Philip II created this army, and Alexander made it even stronger.

Sarissa

Macedonian soldiers carried a **sarissa**, or long spear. They could easily stab an enemy from far away. Macedonian soldiers fought in a phalanx, like the ancient Greeks. The first few rows held out their sarissas, but soldiers who were further back held theirs upwards, to keep them out of the way.

▲ *Sarissas looked like long spears and had sharp points at either end.*

◄ *The cavalry carried spears and a sword into battle.*

Riding high

The hetairoi carried a spear, and wore many kinds of armour. The armour was made of linen and leather, with pieces of metal, like scales, attached. Some wore full metal breastplates to protect the chest.

Armour

Macedonian soldiers wore body armour made of leather. Their shields were smaller and lighter than those of Greek hoplites, which may have made it easier to move.

◄ *Short swords were better for close fighting.*

BATTLE TACTICS

The Macedonian armies of Philip II and Alexander the Great had full-time soldiers, when most other armies had men who fought only part of the time. They were taught how to use weapons effectively and march over long distances.

> *Front lines of soldiers holding their sarissas straight out in front of them helped to stop the enemy from breaking the battle formation.*

Alexander's phalanxes

Alexander used his phalanxes of soldiers to keep the enemy busy fighting at close range. His cavalry tried to chase the enemy cavalry away, leaving the soldiers at both sides of the enemy's army exposed. The cavalry could then charge at any weak areas in the enemy's phalanx and break it up.

In the thick of things

Both Philip II's and Alexander the Great's armies had men who ran out in front of the main army, using weapons such as bows, slings and **javelins** to try and break up the lines.

WARRIOR WISDOM

Alexander's men marched much faster than most armies. Sometimes an enemy surrendered just because they had not expected Alexander to arrive quite so quickly.

ALEXANDER THE GREAT

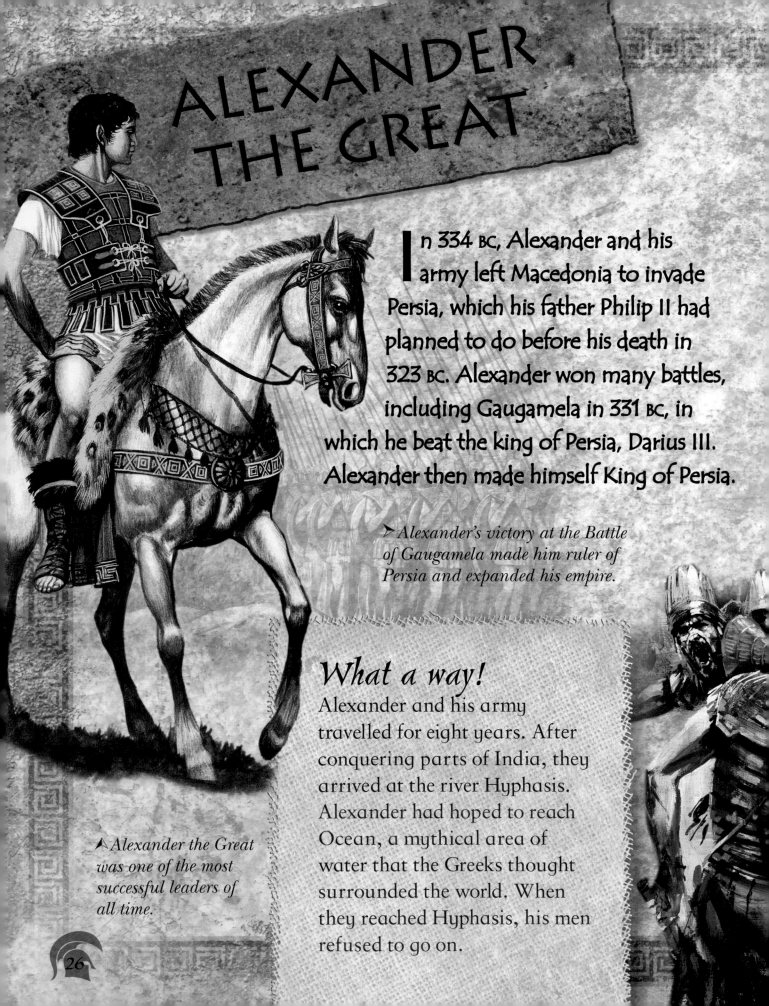

In 334 BC, Alexander and his army left Macedonia to invade Persia, which his father Philip II had planned to do before his death in 323 BC. Alexander won many battles, including Gaugamela in 331 BC, in which he beat the king of Persia, Darius III. Alexander then made himself King of Persia.

➤ *Alexander's victory at the Battle of Gaugamela made him ruler of Persia and expanded his empire.*

What a way!

Alexander and his army travelled for eight years. After conquering parts of India, they arrived at the river Hyphasis. Alexander had hoped to reach Ocean, a mythical area of water that the Greeks thought surrounded the world. When they reached Hyphasis, his men refused to go on.

➤ *Alexander the Great was one of the most successful leaders of all time.*

No heir

Alexander ruled Egypt, western and central Asia and a small part of India. He built a city called Alexandria, named after himself, in Egypt. He had a short life, but he was famous all over the world. Alexander did not have an official **heir** to rule the kingdom after his death. It was divided up into several sections, each ruled by one of his strongest **generals**.

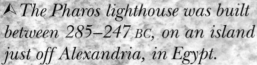 *The Pharos lighthouse was built between 285–247 BC, on an island just off Alexandria, in Egypt.*

WARRIOR WISDOM

Before the Battle of Gaugamela, there was an **eclipse** of the moon. Darius III thought the eclipse was a sign that a warrior from the west was going to rule for eight years. He was right.

THE DECLINE OF ANCIENT GREECE

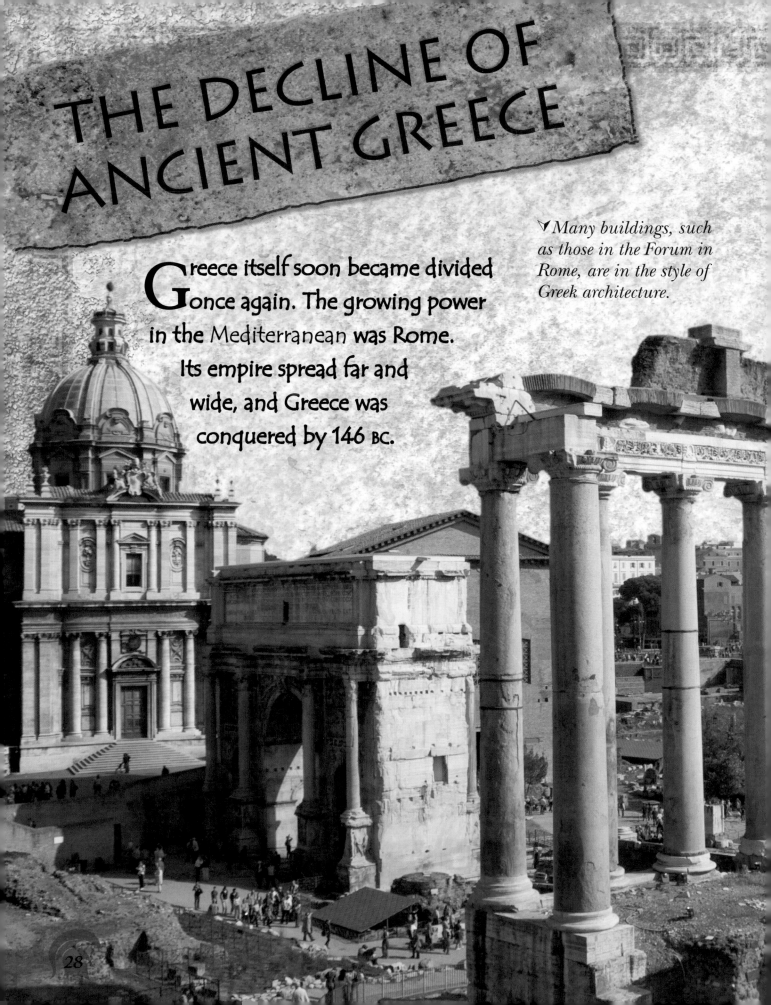

Greece itself soon became divided once again. The growing power in the Mediterranean was Rome. Its empire spread far and wide, and Greece was conquered by 146 BC.

▼Many buildings, such as those in the Forum in Rome, are in the style of Greek architecture.

Greek influence

Alexander spread Greek culture around Asia. He built many cities in which the people followed the Greek way of life. The period from Alexander's death to the beginning of the Roman Empire in 141 BC is known as the **Hellenistic Age**, after the Greeks' name for themselves, Hellenes. The Romans appreciated and learned a lot from Greek culture. The world had moved on, but it was taking Greek ideas with it.

➤ *Life in ancient Greece did not change much after the Romans conquered it in 141 BC.*

Just another day

For most people, the decline of ancient Greece did not make much of a difference to everyday life. Some Greek warriors fought as soldiers for the Roman army, and many others returned to the jobs they had done when they were not fighting.

GLOSSARY

Archer A soldier who fights with a bow and arrows.

Battering ram A large beam used to break down a wall, door or gate of a building.

Bronze A yellow-brown metal made of copper and tin.

Catapult A machine used for throwing stones or other large or heavy objects.

Cavalry Soldiers on horseback.

City-state A city and the surrounding area that forms an independent state.

Crest A ridge or plume sticking up from the top of a helmet.

Cuirass A piece of armour, usually made of bronze that covers the chest.

Eclipse An event in which some or all of the light from the sun or moon is blocked out by another planetary body.

General A leader in an army.

Greave Armour worn on the leg.

Heir A person who has the right to take over the property or position of power from another person once they have died.

Hellenistic Age The period in Greek and Asian history between Alexander the Great's death in 323 BC and the rise of Roman power in 146 BC.

Javelin A lightweight spear.

League A collection of people or countries that work together to help or protect each other against other powers.

Linen A thick material, similar to cotton.

Mediterranean The countries around the Mediterranean Sea.

Phalanx A line formation of soldiers who fought in a tight group with shields overlapping, using spears as weapons.

Rebellion Resistance against a government or ruler of a nation or state.

Region An area in a country or state.

Sarissa A long spear, with points at both ends, carried by Macedonian soldiers.

Siege An attack on a city or building in which the enemy surrounds it, hoping that those inside will surrender.

Sling A weapon made of two cords attached to a pouch, used to throw stones or other objects.

Territory An area belonging to a particular ruler, government or state.

Trireme An ancient Greek ship with sails and three banks of oars.

INDEX

Alexander the Great
    19, 20, 21
    army 22, 24, 25
    empire 26–27, 29
archers 5, 30
armour 4, 10–11, 15,
    16, 23
Athenians 6, 14, 15,
    17, 18, 20

battering rams 12,
    13, 30
bows and arrows 5,
    25

cavalry 19, 21, 23, 24,
    30
city-states 6, 14, 17, 18,
    19, 30

Gaugamela, Battle of
    26, 27
greaves 10, 11
Greek architecture 28

Hellenistic Age 29, 30
helmets 10, 11
hoplites 4, 6, 10, 11
    Battle of Leuctra
        19
    Peloponnesian
        War 18
    Persian War 16
    training 8–9

Ionian Revolt 14, 15

javelins 25, 30

leagues 18, 30
Leuctra, Battle of 19

Macedonians 19, 20,
    22, 23, 24, 25, 26
Marathon, Battle of 7,
    15

Parthenon, Athens 6
Peloponnesian War 18,
    19
Persians 7, 14–15,
    16–17, 26
phalanx 6, 7, 10, 12,
    19, 22, 24, 31
Philip II, King 19, 20,
    21, 22, 24, 25

Romans 28, 29

Salamis, Battle of 17
sarissa 22, 24, 31
shields 6, 9, 10, 11, 16,
    23
ships 12, 13, 17, 18, 31
slings 25, 31
Spartans 5, 6, 8, 9, 14
    Macedonians 20
    Peloponnesian
        War 18
    Persian War 16
    Thebans 19
spears 6, 9, 10, 11, 18,
    30, 31
swords 11, 23

Thebes 19
Thermopylae, Battle of
    16, 17
triremes 13, 31

weapons 4, 10–11,
    30, 31
    Macedonians 24
    machines 12

Xerxes, King 16, 17